SIVA AFI TEINE TOA

By Dahlia Malaeulu
illustrated by Darcy Solia

Teuila watched as the boys warmed up with their wooden sticks. One was concentrating on his grip on the carved wood. Another was using both hands to slowly turn it in front of his body. Then, there was Mika. The best student of them all throwing his stick in the air.

The carved wooden machete that was hanging on the wall above the boys' heads caught Teuila's attention. It was the nifo oti trophy that everyone was competing for.

The day had finally arrived. Teuila had been preparing for the great battle.
Dressed in her siapo, she walked out of the fale Sāmoa to see all the tama toa warriors training.

Some were sparring against each other.

Others were wielding their war clubs around their bodies.

Standing in the middle of them all watching was Mika, who was said to have the strength of a hundred men and was the most feared warrior in the village.

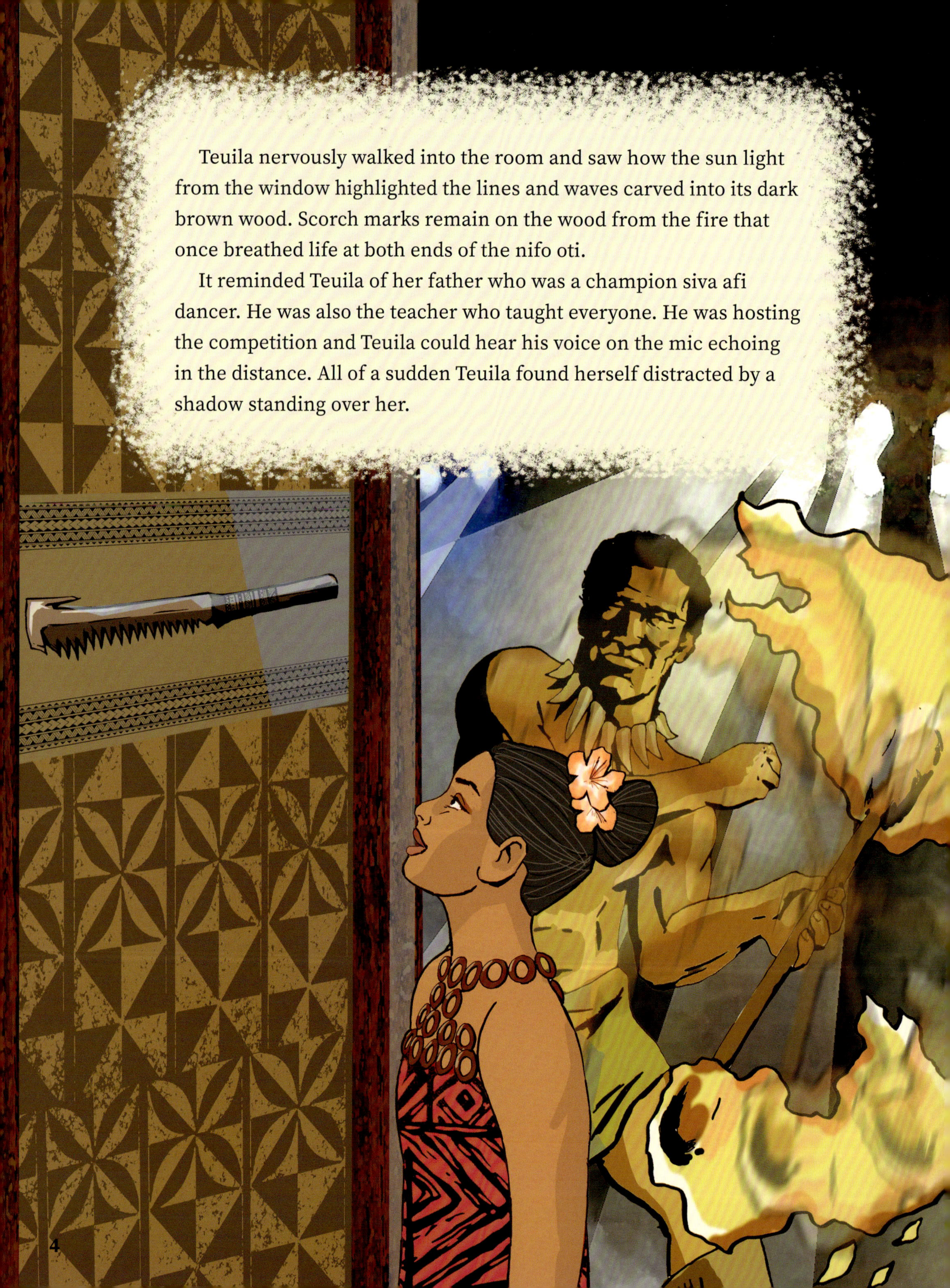

Teuila nervously walked into the room and saw how the sun light from the window highlighted the lines and waves carved into its dark brown wood. Scorch marks remain on the wood from the fire that once breathed life at both ends of the nifo oti.

It reminded Teuila of her father who was a champion siva afi dancer. He was also the teacher who taught everyone. He was hosting the competition and Teuila could hear his voice on the mic echoing in the distance. All of a sudden Teuila found herself distracted by a shadow standing over her.

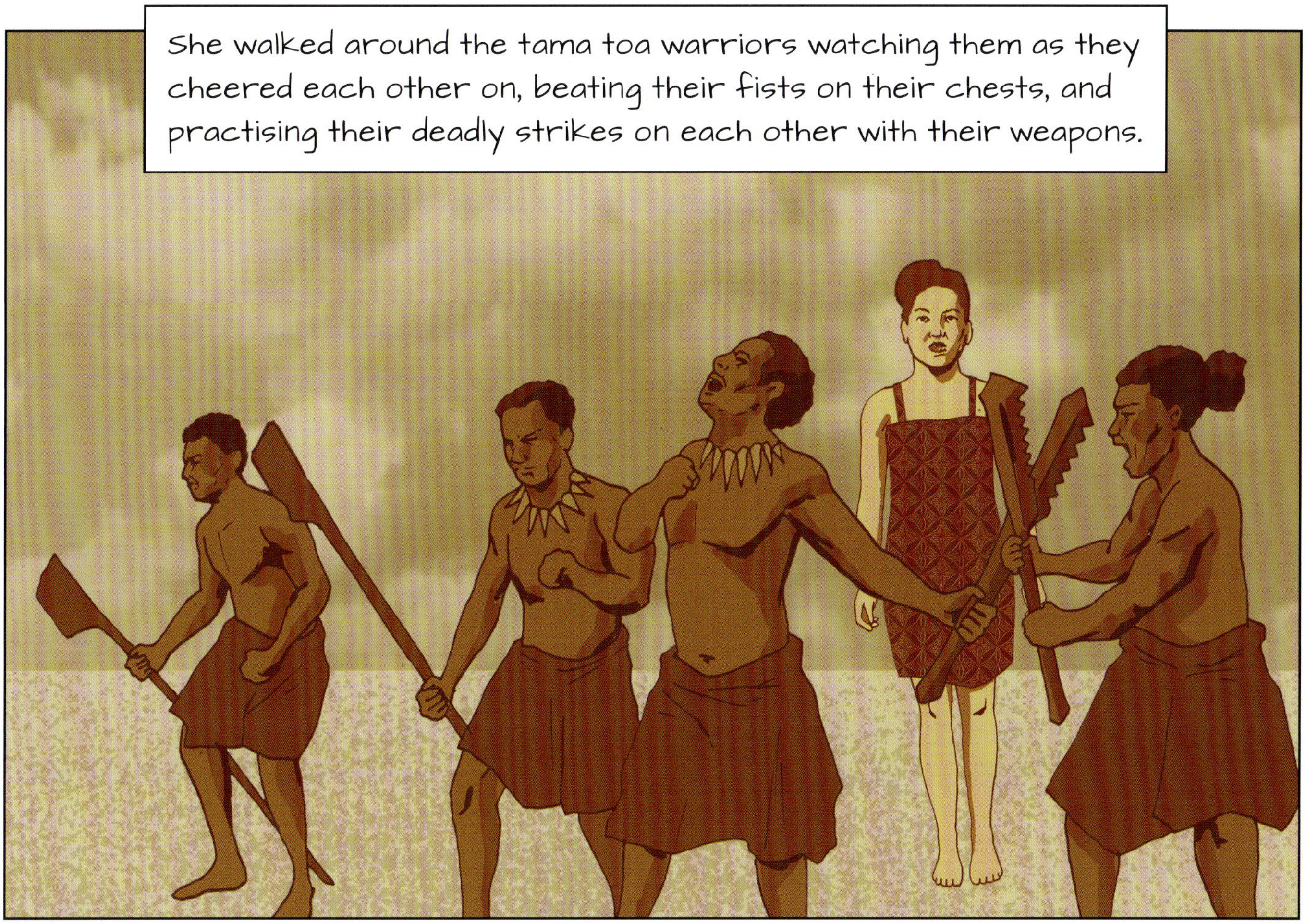

She walked around the tama toa warriors watching them as they cheered each other on, beating their fists on their chests, and practising their deadly strikes on each other with their weapons.

Teuila had been instructed to make her way to the fale Sāmoa where the matai gathered.

Teuila heard a joking voice say, “It’s not too late to enter into the siva Sāmoa competition.” She turned to find Mika standing behind her. He was known to give everyone a hard time, especially Teuila who was the only girl competing for his title.

It was the first time girls had been allowed to enter. Last year Mika had won the siva afi competition and was presented with the special nifo oti trophy. He would be defending his title, but this year’s competition was different.

How can you lead us into battle little girl?

Maybe he was right?

Teuila shook her head to chase her thoughts away as her and Mika were ushered into the fale Sāmoa.

The matai had finished their traditional 'ava ceremony which included blessings and well wishes for the battle that was about to begin. They sat around in a circle, each person in front of a post.

Suddenly, Teuila noticed something very different about the new Ali'i, paramount chief.

Mika looked on silently examining his general.

As the seated matai started leaving the fale Sāmoa, Teuila saw that the stories from the village were true about this new ali'i chief called Nafanua.

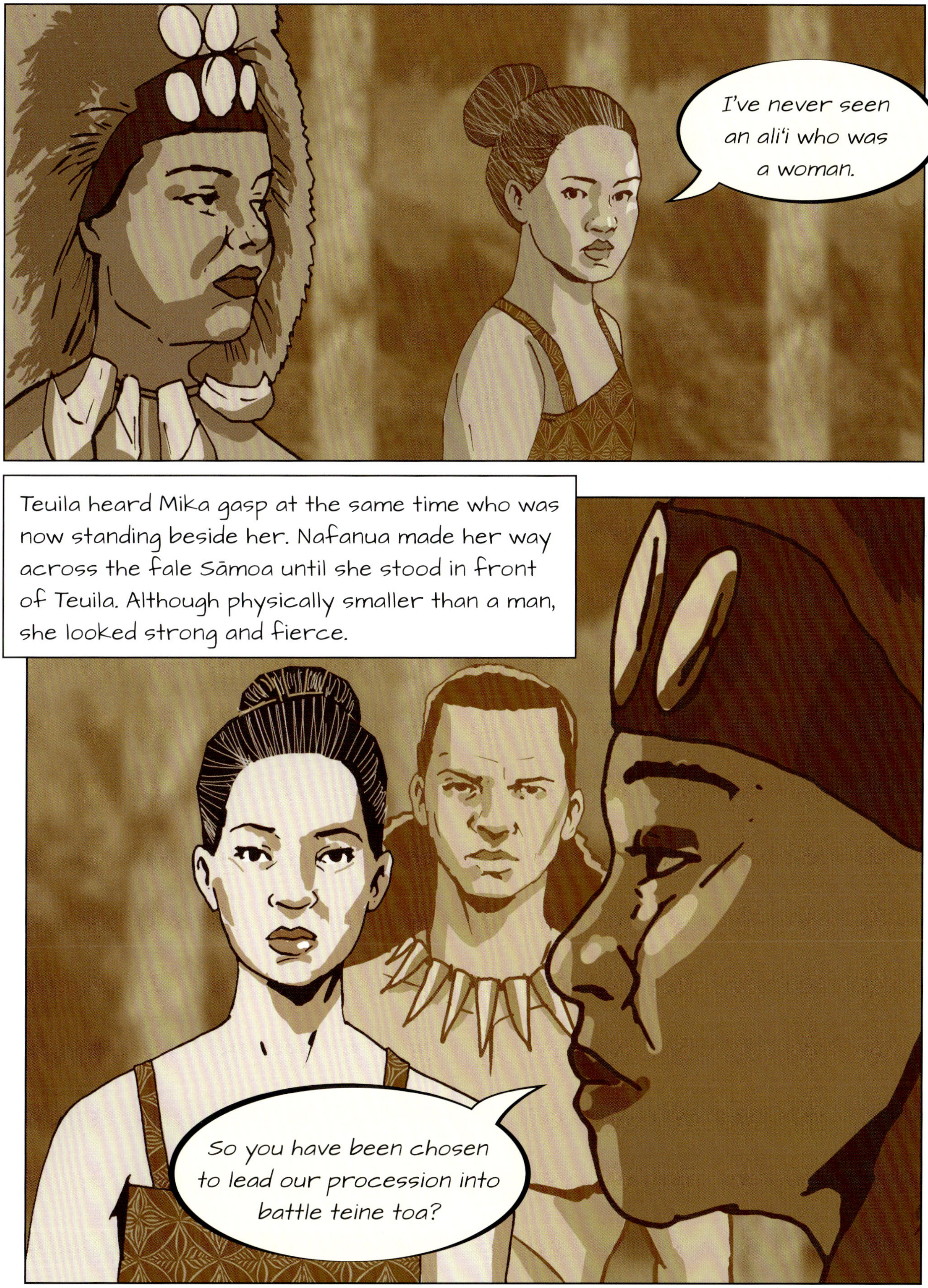

Teuila heard Mika gasp at the same time who was now standing beside her. Nafanua made her way across the fale Sāmoa until she stood in front of Teuila. Although physically smaller than a man, she looked strong and fierce.

So you have been chosen to lead our procession into battle teine toa?

Teuila was glad to have her own space away from the other boy competitors. She saw her mother walking towards her with a clipboard in hand. She was in charge of the backstage.

"Are you ready?" Her mother asked. She could tell something was wrong.

Teuila looked at her mother.

"Maybe I should have entered the siva Sāmoa competition mum and left the siva afi to the boys." Teuila's mother gave her a hug and sat her down wanting to mend her broken spirit. She was Teuila's siva Sāmoa teacher. She looked at her daughter.

"Why do you think taupou dance with nifo oti for the taualuga?" She asked Teuila. Teuila shrugged her shoulders, looking down at her feet. She muttered "I don't know."

Teuila's mother explained, "Did you know that women, including taupou, did siva afi or 'ailao afi? They used to wrap both ends of the nifo oti with bandages and set them on fire ... Long ago, teine toa helped to lead tama toa into battle too. This is why taupou dance with nifo oti."

Teuila's mother reached into Teuila's bag and pulled out the bandaged nifo oti that had been gifted to her and passed down in their family. Teuila's mother stood up and with both hands she slowly started turning the nifo oti in front of her, focusing on her hands as she turned it faster and faster until she threw it into the air above her head. The nifo oti turned like an out of control bicycle wheel only stopping when her mother caught it. Teuila stood in amazement as her mother paused, holding the nifo oti in front of her daughter saying, "It is already in us. You deserve to be here. We are teine toa."

Nafanua took Teuila's nifo oti and ordered both ends to be lit on fire. As they were set alight Nafanua said ...

I see waves of red, yellow, orange. Dancing flames burning hot, short and violent, igniting the night, outshining the stars. With no care of what will be left behind. I tame the heat and breathe life into the light. I am fire.

With one hand she slowly turned the nifo oti and threw it in the air.

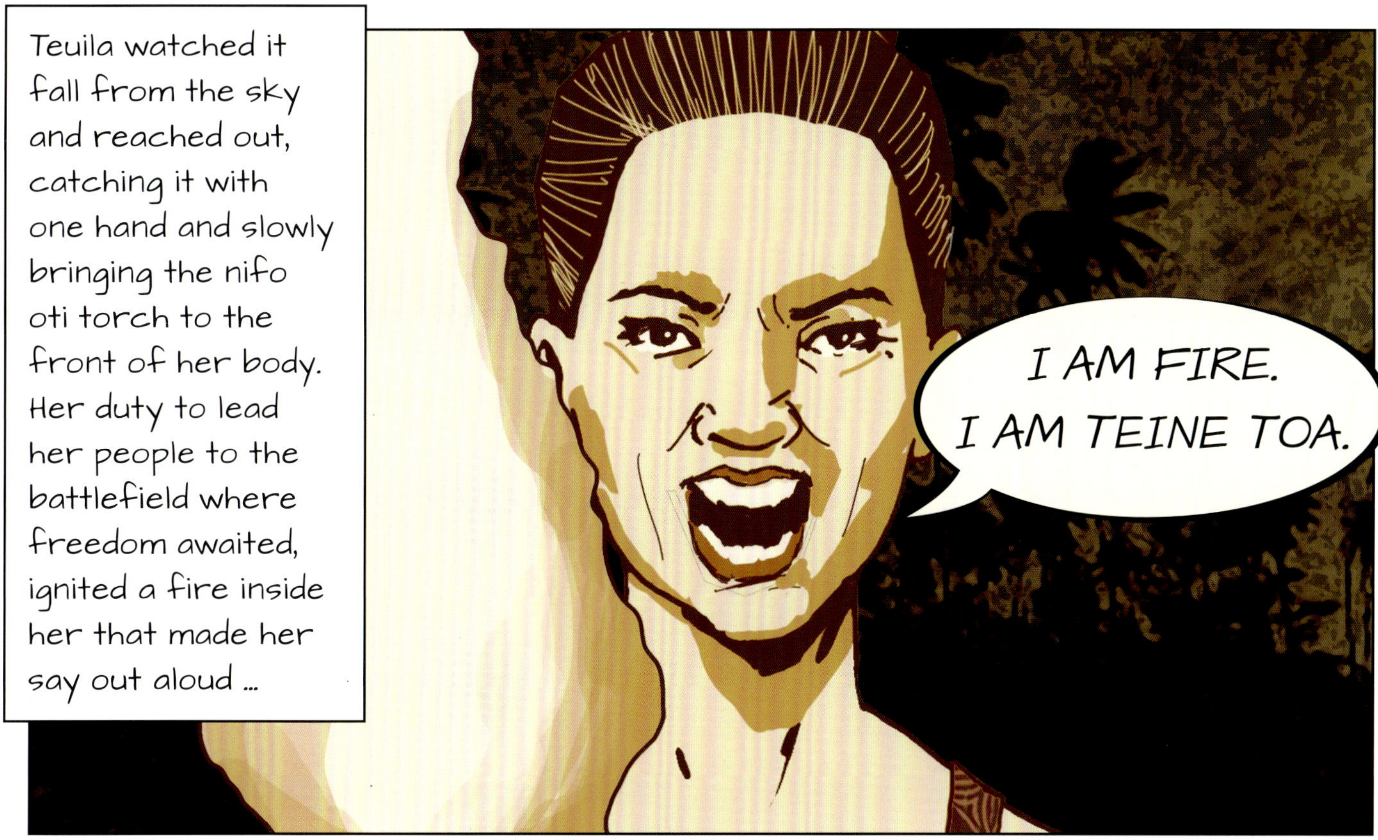

Teuila watched it fall from the sky and reached out, catching it with one hand and slowly bringing the nifo oti torch to the front of her body. Her duty to lead her people to the battlefield where freedom awaited, ignited a fire inside her that made her say out aloud ...

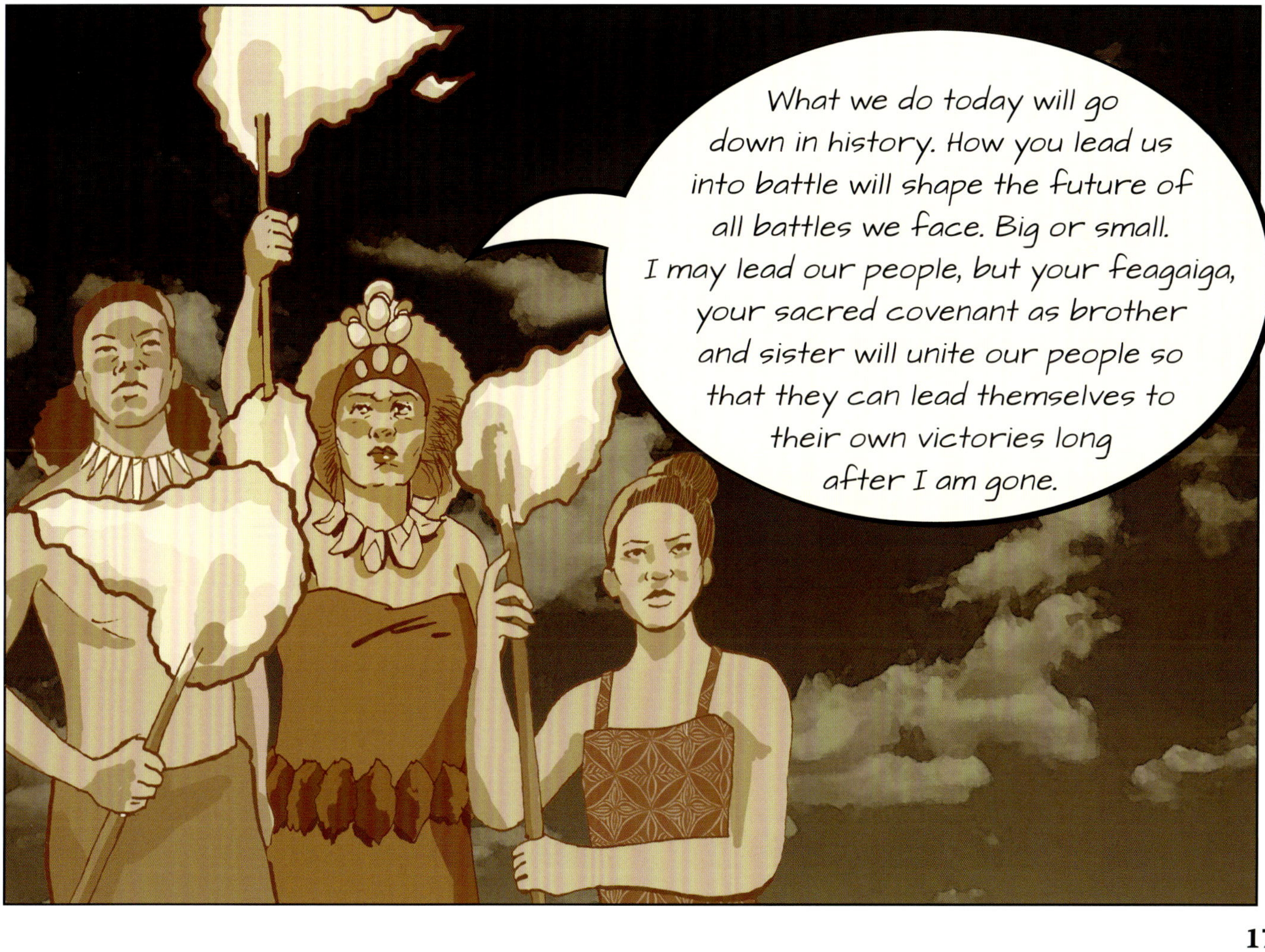

What we do today will go down in history. How you lead us into battle will shape the future of all battles we face. Big or small. I may lead our people, but your feagaiga, your sacred covenant as brother and sister will unite our people so that they can lead themselves to their own victories long after I am gone.

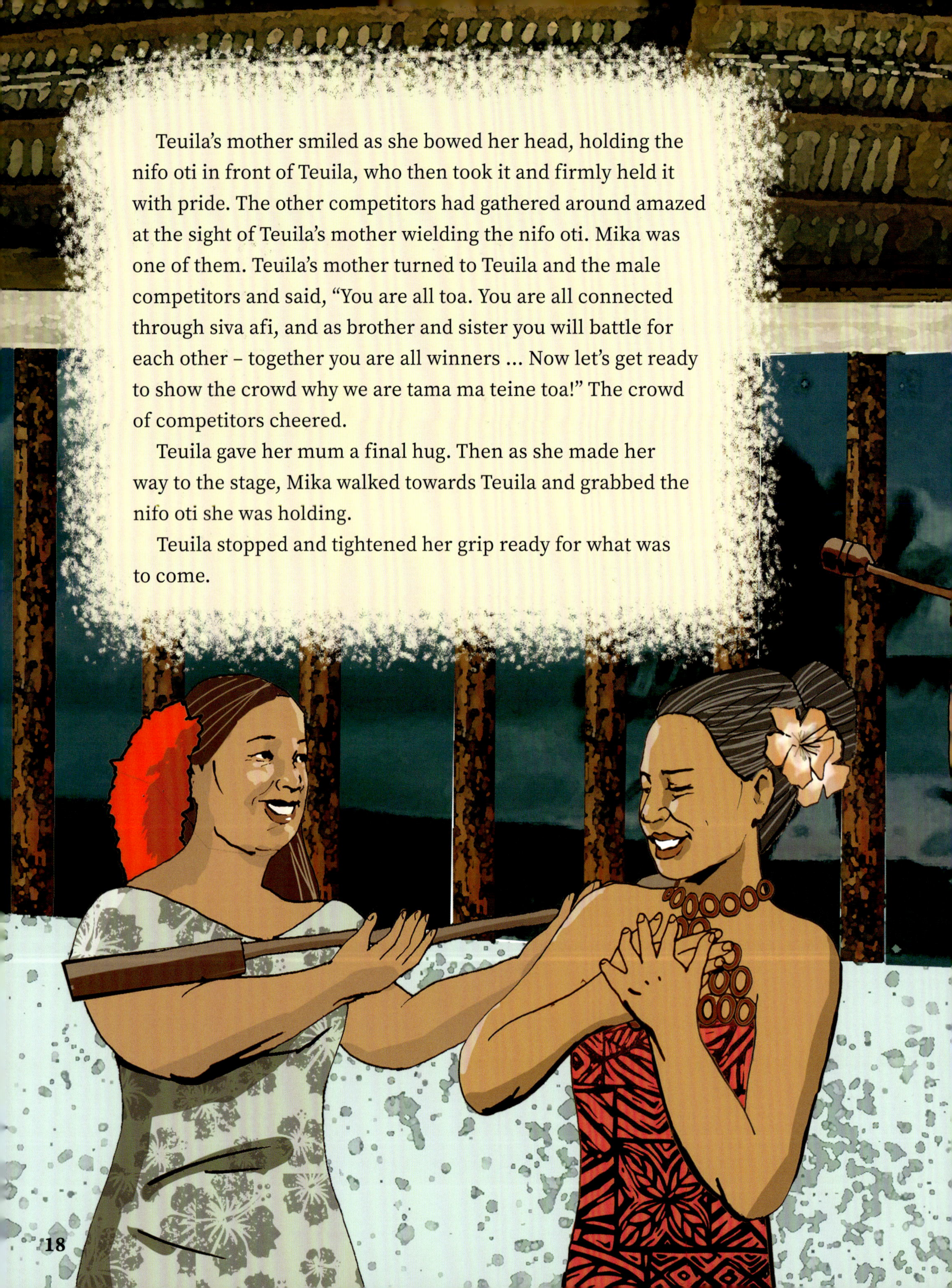

Teuila's mother smiled as she bowed her head, holding the nifo oti in front of Teuila, who then took it and firmly held it with pride. The other competitors had gathered around amazed at the sight of Teuila's mother wielding the nifo oti. Mika was one of them. Teuila's mother turned to Teuila and the male competitors and said, "You are all toa. You are all connected through siva afi, and as brother and sister you will battle for each other – together you are all winners ... Now let's get ready to show the crowd why we are tama ma teine toa!" The crowd of competitors cheered.

Teuila gave her mum a final hug. Then as she made her way to the stage, Mika walked towards Teuila and grabbed the nifo oti she was holding.

Teuila stopped and tightened her grip ready for what was to come.

WE ARE TOA!
... Mika yelled at the top of his lungs holding his war club above his head. Suddenly the fale Sāmoa was surrounded by tama toa banging and hitting the sides of the fale Sāmoa with their fists and war clubs chanting ...
WE ARE TOA!
WE ARE TOA!
WE ARE TOA!

Hypnotised by the golden balls of fire at the end of her nifo oti, other tama toa joined Teuila. Fire danced furiously across the sky. Together, with Mika they walked towards the boundary of their village. Mika then paused, turned to Teuila and said, "You are teine toa." Teuila replied with Nafanua's spirit in her eyes ...
WE ARE FIRE!

Mika released his grip and said, “Sorry about before sis and good luck teine toa.”

Feeling relieved, Teuila loosened her grip and smiled, “You too, tama toa.”

Teuila slowly made her way up the steps of the stage. Her father’s voice proudly announced her name into the mic. The drums started. The crowd roared. Teuila lit her nifo oti, which she held in front of her body. She watched the red, yellow and orange flames dance excitedly.

Teuila felt different. She felt stronger, empowered by something that seemed to be fuelled by the teine toa spirit that had been inside her all along.

Teuila paused and stood in the middle of the stage. She quietened the crowd by holding the nifo oti above her head. That’s when she heard a familiar voice whisper -

“You are fire. You are teine toa.”

- Siva afi is performed by women and men and is also known as ʻailao afi.
- Traditionally, ʻailao afi was when Samoan warriors displayed their strength through artful twirling, throwing, catching and dancing with a war club.
- The nifo oti is a serrated-edged Samoan war club. War clubs like the nifo oti, were traditionally used by toa warriors in the art of hand to hand combat.
- Nafanua was the war goddess of Sāmoa. She is known for winning the battle between Aʻea i Sasaʻe and Aʻea i Sisifo, where she fought like a man, but surprised her enemies when she revealed that she was a woman.
- In Samoan culture the brother-sister feagaiga or sacred covenant is a lifelong commitment, where the brother respects, protects and honours his sister. This respect extends to all women, and is the meaning behind the Samoan saying, "O le iʻo i mata o le tama o le teine" - The pupil of the brother's eye is his sister.
- Siva afi today is mostly performed for entertainment and annual fire knife dance competitions are held at the Polynesian Cultural Centre in Hawaii.